Lions

Lions

Sandra Lee

THE CHILD'S WORLD®, INC.

Published in the United States of America by The Child's World®, Inc.
PO Box 326
Chanhassen, MN 55317-0326
800-599-READ
www.childsworld.com

Product Manager Mary Berendes
Editor Katherine Stevenson
Designer Mary Berendes
Contributor Bob Temple

Photo Credits
© 1998 Adam Jones/Dembinsky Photo Assoc. Inc.: 20
© 1997 Anup Shah/Dembinsky Photo Assoc. Inc.: 24
© Barbara Gerlach/Visuals Unlimited: 10
© Catherine Gehm: 19
© 1995 Craig Brandt: 23
© 1999 E. R. Degginger/Dembinsky Photo Assoc. Inc.: 6
© Erwin and Peggy Bauer: 15
© Fritz Polking/Visuals Unlimited: 2
© Joe McDonald/Visuals Unlimited: 26
© Leonard Lee Rue III: cover
© 1994 Mark J. Thomas/Dembinsky Photo Assoc. Inc.: 16
© 2001 Renee Lynn/Stone: 29
© 1999 Robin Brandt: 13
© 2001 Tim Davis/Stone: 9
© Wolfgang Kaehler 2001 www.wkaehlerphoto.com: 30

Library of Congress Cataloging-in-Publication Data
Lee, Sandra.
Lions / by Sandra Lee.
p. cm.
Includes index.
ISBN 1-56766-887-9 (library bound : alk. paper)
1. Lions—Juvenile literature. [1. Lions.] I. Title.
QL737.C23 L44 2001
599.757—dc21
00-010772

On the cover...

Front cover: This male lion is resting in some tall grass in Africa.
Page 2: This lioness is watching some animals across a field in Kenya.

Table of Contents

Nighttime on the African plains isn't as peaceful as people might think. Many animals are busy eating and drinking. In the darkness, one animal quietly waits to catch its evening meal. It is a big cat with golden hair and golden eyes. In the distance, relatives of this big cat call out to each other with a deep, throaty cry. What are these wild cats? They're lions!

⇐ You can see this lioness's glowing eyes as she hunts at night in Botswana.

What Are Lions?

Lions are one of the biggest and most powerful members of the cat family. Their muscular shoulders and legs give them strength for hunting. A male lion can weigh up to 500 pounds. It is nearly 4 feet tall at the shoulder and about 10 feet long from nose to tail. A female lion, called a **lioness,** is slightly smaller.

This huge male is running toward the photographer. ⇒

A male lion has a collar of hair surrounding his face. This long, thick hair is called a **mane.** The mane makes the lion look even bigger and stronger than he really is. It also protects him from scratches and bites when he fights. A lion's mane can be golden, brown, or black. Most are a mixture of these colors.

Both male and female lions have four muscular legs with large paws. They use these paws to knock down food animals as they try to run away. Like most other cats, lions have whiskers on their faces and long, thin tails. And of course, lions have powerful jaws and very sharp teeth!

⇐ You can see this male's beautiful mane as he rests in a New Mexico zoo.

Where Do Lions Live?

Long ago, lions ranged from Europe to Africa to Asia. Today, they live on the grassy plains of eastern and central Africa and in India. Thousands of lions also live in zoos throughout the world. In captivity, lions can live to be about 30 years old. In the wild, most live to be about 8 to 10 years old.

This wild lioness is hunting in some tall grass in Botswana. ⇒

Do Lions Live Alone?

In the wild, lions live in family groups called **prides.** Prides can have 10 to 20 lions, or even as many as 35. Each pride is made up of one to three adult males, several lionesses, and young lions called **cubs.** Life within the pride is peaceful. When a member returns after an absence, the lions greet each other by rubbing cheeks. Cubs chase each other and wrestle playfully. The lions usually spend about 20 hours a day resting and sleeping.

Many of the lions in this pride are cubs. One adult ⇒ lioness is in this picture. Can you find her?

Each pride stays within a certain area called a **territory.** The territory contains the food and water the lions need to survive. If they need more food, the lions make their territory larger. The lions don't allow strange lions or other animals to hunt in their territory. The male lions keep intruders out by roaring. They also mark the edges of their territory with scents. Their roaring and scents tell strangers to stay away—or be attacked.

Sometimes lions want to smell things even better. To do this, they use a special area on the roof of their mouth called a **Jacobson's organ.** To use this organ, a lion opens its mouth and pulls back its lips. It almost looks as if it's smiling! This funny-looking behavior is called the *Flehmen* movement.

⇐ This male is using the Flehmen movement to detect the scents on this bush.

Pride members stay together for years, except for the males. When male cubs are between two and three years old, their father chases them from the territory. The young males wander alone until they are fully grown. Then they may fight a male from another pride. If they win, they take over that pride's territory and lionesses.

These two males are fighting on the ⇒
Masai Mara Game Reserve in Kenya.

What Are Baby Lions Like?

A lioness gives birth to one to four cubs at a time. The newborn babies are blind and helpless. They depend on their mother for everything—especially food. The babies drink their mother's milk and spend much of their time sleeping. As they get older, the cubs can be a handful as they play and wrestle. The lionesses in each pride share the work of raising the cubs. Cubs often get their milk from other lionesses as well as their own mother.

⇐ This young cub is resting on a log in Kenya.

How Do Lions Hunt?

Lions are **predators,** which means they kill and eat other animals. They prefer to hunt large animals such as zebras, antelope, wildebeests, and buffalo. Most of these animals are faster than the lions, so the lions must creep up on them and surprise them. The color of a lion's coat is ideal for hiding. It is yellowish brown, the same color as the grass on the African plains.

This young male is watching a nearby herd of wildebeests. ⇒
He is choosing which one he will attack.

The lionesses do most of the pride's hunting. They hunt at night so they can sneak up on their victims, or **prey.** Sometimes lionesses hunt alone. Often they hunt together and share the food once they kill their prey. Lions hear and smell very well. They wait in the long grass until their prey is close. Then they charge at the animal full speed. The lion uses its huge paws to knock the prey down and then quickly grasps the animal by the throat or face. When the prey animal runs out of air, it dies.

⇐ This lioness has caught a Cape buffalo. She has wrapped her mouth around the buffalo's mouth and nose so it cannot breathe.

After killing its prey, the lion drags the animal back to the pride. Then all the lions stuff themselves with food. A male can eat 75 pounds of meat in one meal! Lions have 30 teeth, but they don't use them for chewing. Instead, they use their teeth to hold and tear the meat. They swallow their food in chunks.

Do Lions Have Enemies?

Because of their size and strength, lions have no natural enemies—just people. As people move into lions' territories to live, the lions sometimes kill cows, goats, and even people for food. So people kill the lions to protect their property. Other people hunt lions for sport.

This angry male does not want to be bothered. ⇒

Today, most lions live in national parks and **reserves,** where they are protected from hunters. Here they have large areas in which to roam, sleep, and raise their young. Many people now travel to Africa to learn about lions and take pictures of them instead of shooting them. Perhaps some day you will be able to visit Africa and see these spectacular cats in the wild!

Glossary

cubs (KUBZ)
Baby lions are called cubs. Lionesses work together to raise their cubs.

Jacobson's organ (JAY-kub-sonz OR-gen)
A Jacobson's organ is an area on certain animals that help them to smell things better. Lions make the Flehmen movement when they use their Jacobson's organ.

lioness (LY-un-ess)
A female lion is called a lioness. Lionesses often hunt together.

mane (MANE)
A mane is an area of long, thick hair around an animal's head. Male lions have a mane.

predators (PREH-deh-terz)
Predators are animals that kill and eat other animals. Lions are predators.

prey (PRAY)
Animals that are killed and eaten by other animals are called prey. Many animals are prey for lions.

prides (PRYDZ)
Prides are groups of lions that live together. A pride can include 10 or more lions.

reserves (ree-ZERVZ)
Reserves are protected areas of land set aside for animals to live. Most lions live in reserves.

territory (TEHR-ih-tor-ee)
A territory is an area an animal claims as its own. Each pride of lions has its own territory.

Web Sites

http://www.thebigzoo.com/Animals/African_lion.asp

http://www.awf.org/animals/lion.html

http://www.lionlmb.org/lion/lionfact.html